American Library Association
"Top Ten Religion Books for Youth"
Booklist

TOUGH QUESTIONS JEWS ASK

A Young Adult's Guide to Building a Jewish Life

W9-BEQ-755

2ND EDITION

RABBI EDWARD FEINSTEIN

JEWISH LIGHTS Publishing
Woodstock, Vermont

Tough Questions Jews Ask, 2nd Edition:
A Young Adult's Guide to Building a Jewish Life

2012 Quality Paperback Edition, First Printing
© 2012 by Edward Feinstein

Library of Congress Cataloging-in-Publication Data
Feinstein, Edward, 1954–
Tough questions Jews ask : a young adult's guide to building a Jewish life / Edward Feinstein. — 2nd ed.
  p. cm.
Includes bibliographical references.
ISBN 978-1-58023-454-2 (quality pbk. original) 1. Jewish way of life—Juvenile literature. 2. Judaism—Customs and practices—Juvenile literature. I. Title.
BM723.F43 2012
296.70835—dc23
2011047362

10 9 8 7 6 5 4 3 2 1

Manufactured in the United States of America

Cover Design: Bronwen Battaglia

Published by Jewish Lights Publishing
A Division of LongHill Partners, Inc.
Sunset Farm Offices, Route 4, P.O. Box 237
Woodstock, VT 05091
Tel: (802) 457-4000 Fax: (802) 457-4004
www.jewishlights.com

Contents

Preface to the Second Edition

What's new in this new edition? Based on the wonderful reactions from so many readers since *Tough Questions Jews Ask* was first published, and changes that have taken place among Jewish teens, I've added three new questions to this new edition that today's teens are grappling with. Together, we take a look at the pros and cons of the new powerful ways we have of communicating, and show why face-to-face communication is still the most meaningful. We learn why the Torah forbids Jews to get tattoos and body piercings, and how making your mark through kind actions can be a much more powerful symbol of individuality. We also explore the religion of Islam, dispel some myths, and identify some similarities between the Muslim faith and Judaism. I hope you'll find the new material even more relevant to your needs, whether as a teen student or as a teacher or parent. If you would like to share your reactions to the new material with me, please send me an e-mail at efeinstein@vbs.org.

How to Read This Book

I've always had lots of questions—tough questions, the kind of questions that just won't go away. Even though I had wonderful teachers growing up, teachers who listened patiently and tried to help me find answers, my list of questions just kept growing. (Good questions never go away.) One of the reasons I started studying to be a rabbi was to find answers to my own questions.

When I became a rabbi, I promised myself that I would never turn away anyone who had a good question. And so, for more than twenty years I've been listening to questions— from kids and adults, from teens and seniors, from Christians and Jews. Some questions have easy answers. Most of the really good questions can't be answered at all. I've tried to help people think about their questions and seek out their own answers.

This book is a collection of some of the best questions I've been asked and the responses that have helped people think more deeply. To make it fun, I imagined that the people who asked the best questions were all in one class. So the class I describe here is made up, but the questions are real and the people who asked are real. (I changed their names to keep their parents from getting mad at them for giving the rabbi a hard time!)

You can read the chapters in order, or you can skip around. You might want to keep a log of your own answers to the questions and a list of new questions that come up as you're reading.

As you read this book, please remember that there are many, many different ways to be Jewish. There are many different ways to understand and practice the Jewish religion. There are many ways to come close to God. There are many ways to answer life's toughest questions. We Jews are like a family sharing conversation at the dinner table. There is never only one right opinion, never only one way to be Jewish. These answers are one person's ideas and interpretations. I'm a rabbi, and I've spent a great deal of time thinking and learning about these things, but I'm still just one person. You can agree or disagree with me; you can argue with me. (In fact, I hope you will.) Your parents, your teachers, even other rabbis may have completely different answers to the questions. I hope you'll go and ask them to share their ideas. Most of all, I hope you will never stop asking. I believe that God loves good questions.

 *Acknowledgments*

I am grateful to all those who have asked me tough questions over the years, including the kids, staff, and families of the Solomon Schechter Academy of Dallas, where I was principal; Congregation Shearith Israel, where I was rabbi; Camp Ramah in California, where I was the director; the Ziegler Rabbinical School of American Jewish University, where I teach; and Valley Beth Shalom, where I'm a rabbi.

I have been very fortunate over the years to have many loving teachers who listened to my endless questions. These include Rabbi Elijah J. Schochet, Professor Elliot N. Dorff, Professor Neil Gillman, Rabbi David Hartman, and my mentor, Rabbi Harold M. Schulweis. I've been blessed with loving colleagues and friends who have helped me seek the answers. I am grateful to every one of them for sharing their wisdom and support.

I thank my editor, Bryna Fischer, for her help and patience. I thank Stuart M. Matlins, publisher, and the people at Jewish Lights for making this book and so many works of light and wisdom accessible to thinking, seeking souls.

And I thank God for the blessing of a loving family; for my parents, Dov and Chaiky, *z"l*, Herb and Geri; for our kids, Yonah, Nessa and Daniel, and Raffi; and for Nina, who has answered so many of my questions.

1

Am I Allowed to Ask?

DOES IT MAKE GOD MAD IF WE ASK QUESTIONS?

They were the worst class anyone could remember. "Teacher-slayers," they were called. It was only December and already they had sent three teachers into early retirement. Mrs. Goldenberg, a veteran of years of teaching seventh grade, left after a month of their rude behavior and cruel practical jokes. Mr. Weinberg presented himself as a "cool" young teacher who rode a motorcycle to the synagogue and quoted lyrics from the latest songs. He lasted a week and a half. Ms. Alon, once a sergeant in the Israeli army, had survived real terrorists, but she couldn't survive this class.

I was the last resort. I'm the rabbi. I'm supposed to know how to perform miracles.

I suppose it was something of a miracle that happened. The kids in the class realized that it was one thing to knock off a few ordinary teachers; it was quite another thing to get on the wrong side of your rabbi. After all, they all looked forward to celebrating a Bar or Bat Mitzvah in the coming year. And for that, you need the rabbi.

When I walked into the room, they were ready. Not with their usual greeting of foul words, bored looks, spitballs, and paper airplanes, but with a sort of petition.

Dear Rabbi,

As you know, this is our graduating year in the Hebrew School. But we still have lots of questions that never got answered in the years we've been here. Instead of learning the stuff in the book, could we please spend the time we have left this year answering these questions?

Respectfully,

The Seventh Grade Class

"Sounds like a great idea," I responded. "Let's begin right away. I'll try to answer any questions you have. What's your first one?"

There was a moment of silence, as if they hadn't really expected me to go along with the idea. And then the girl who handed me the petition said softly, "I have lots of questions about God and stuff, but I'm afraid if I tell you, you won't let me have my Bat Mitzvah. So I wonder, are we really allowed to ask you questions? Does it make God mad if we ask questions?"

That's how we started.

Let me tell you about my Bar Mitzvah. The week before my Bar Mitzvah, I was a mess. I had just turned thirteen. I was becoming an adult, or so everyone was telling me. I was scheduled to stand up in front of the rabbi, my family, and the congregation and tell everyone how proud I was to be Jewish. But I was so full of questions! *Why* am I Jewish? Do I really believe in all this? Do I really believe in God? Do I believe the stories in the Torah or the words of the prayer book? How can I believe God exists if the world is so full of suffering? Who needs a Bar Mitzvah, anyway? How can I honestly go through with a Bar Mitzvah if I'm so full of questions?

I had an uncle who was an important rabbi. He spent a lifetime learning and teaching Torah at an Orthodox college in Chicago. Just before my Bar Mitzvah, he moved to Los Angeles, where we lived. My father thought it would be a good idea for me to meet Uncle Mottel. So Dad drove me to Uncle Mottel's apartment, introduced me, then disappeared.

I sat, trembling, in front of my uncle. He asked me about my studies and how I'd prepared for my Bar Mitzvah. I told him what I'd learned. And then from somewhere deep in me came something I hadn't meant to say, "Uncle Mottel, do you ever have questions that just won't go away? Do you ever wonder if God is real? Do you ever wonder if the Torah is true? Do you ever wonder why you're Jewish?"

For a moment, I was embarrassed and scared. Maybe he'd get mad and throw me out! Maybe he'd recite some ancient curse and turn me into a worm! Maybe he'd cancel my Bar Mitzvah and expel me from the Jewish people. But Uncle Mottel smiled kindly and answered softly, "Do I have questions? Do I wonder about God? Every single day! Every day I wonder if God is real, if the Torah is true. Every day I wonder why I'm a Jew. But that's part of being Jewish. In the Torah, we're called *Yisrael*—the ones who wrestle with God. Wrestling, asking, wondering, searching is just what God wants us to do! God loves good questions! Now tell me, what are your questions?" He listened with patience and concentration.

We spent two hours and a whole six-pack of soda talking through my questions and his questions, his answers and my answers. Every question brought an answer. And every answer brought a new question. He pulled down dozens of old books filled with wisdom—the Bible, volumes of the Talmud, and books of Hasidic stories. "Study these books," he instructed me. "You will find many others who asked your questions. Study these books and join their discussion! That's what it means to be *Yisrael*, to be a Jew."

A week later, I stood on the *bimah* of the synagogue for my Bar Mitzvah. I was nervous. After all, every kid from my class was there! But I wasn't worried about my questions any longer. Uncle Mottel had invited me to wonder, to ask questions, to join the discussion of those who have spent more than three thousand years wondering and asking—the Jewish people, my people.

In Judaism, you're allowed to ask questions. You're invited to ask questions. In fact, asking questions is about the most important thing Jewish people do. In the Bible, Abraham, the first Jew, asks God a zinger of a question: "How can You, the Judge of all the earth, not do what's right?" (Genesis 18:25). The most important moment in the Passover seder is the asking of a question: "Why is tonight different from all other nights?" The Talmud, the great encyclopedia of Jewish wisdom, teaches that if you're too embarrassed to ask questions, you'll never learn anything (*Pirke* Avot 2:5).

Why are questions so important? Because we're Jewish with our entire self—our thoughts, our feelings, and our actions. We're not allowed to leave out any part of ourselves. The Torah teaches, "You will love the Lord your God with all your heart, with all your life, and with all your strength" (Deuteronomy 6:5). Notice the word "all." Your whole self must be involved. You're not allowed to believe in something that makes no sense to you. You're not allowed to do things that feel wrong to you. Thinking, feeling, believing, and doing must be whole. People get into trouble when they feel without thinking, believe without thinking, or do without thinking. If it doesn't make sense—ask! If it doesn't feel right—ask! As a Jew, that's what is expected of you!

2

Who Believes in God Anymore?

WHY SHOULD I BELIEVE IN GOD? WHY SHOULD ANYONE?

Billy was acknowledged by everyone to be the smartest kid in the class. For fun, he tore apart computers and put them together again. He spent most of his Hebrew School hours reading science fiction. But with the rabbi in the room, he saw a chance to set a few things straight.

"Rabbi, I believe in science. I believe in evolution. I believe in nature. But I don't believe in God. Why should I believe in God? Why should anyone?"

A rabbi I know once asked a class of teenagers, "How many of you believe in God?" Not one hand went up.

"Rabbi, no one believes in God anymore!" they explained.

The rabbi was heartbroken. These were great kids. They were involved in the life of his synagogue. "How could they not believe in God?" he wondered. So he spent the rest of the class trying to convince them. He showed them all sorts of impressive philosophical proofs and arguments. But at the end of the class, the kids said to him, "Nice try, Rabbi. But we still don't believe in God."

The rabbi went home that night with a terrible headache. This class really depressed him. He met with the class again the following week. This time, he asked a different question: "When in your life did you ever feel that God was close to you?"

Every kid in the class had an answer.

One boy said, "Every Friday night, my mom lights candles for Shabbat. She says a quiet prayer and her eyes get filled up with tears. And somehow I know that God is listening to her prayers."

Another student said, "When my grandfather died, the whole family came to the cemetery. We all stood around his grave and told stories of his life. Somehow, I knew that God was close then."

A girl said, "Last summer, my family took a trip to Israel. At the same time that our plane landed, a plane of Jews from Russia or someplace also landed. Those people were so glad to get to Israel that they got down on their knees and kissed the ground. At that moment, I knew that God was close."

Have you ever felt that God was close to you? I think that at some time or another, almost everyone has had a feeling that God is close. These are often the most power-ful moments in our lives. These are the moments that let us know that our lives are very special. We may not know what God is. We may not have words to describe God. But we have a strong sense that God is close.

Several years ago, I was diagnosed with cancer. My doctors told me that I might not have long to live. An emer-gency operation was followed by months of very unpleas-ant medicine. This was the most terrifying time in my life. I started to wonder if there was a God who cared for me. And then I met Charles. Charles was a night nurse in the hospital. He and I came from different worlds: I'm a Jew from California; he's an African American Baptist from Alabama. But each night, Charles came to my hospital room to care for me. When I complained, which I did a lot, he told me jokes. When I was in pain, he made me feel better. When I didn't want to take my medicine, he yelled at me. When I was scared, he gave me strength and inspiration. Each morning, he came one last time to check on me and leave me with a thought for the day. "You have faith now, Rabbi!" he would say. No amount of money in the world could pay Charles for what he did for me. And as I fought this cancer, I discovered that the world is filled with people like Charles. This may be what the Bible means when it says that people are "created in God's image" (Genesis 1:27). Through their kindness, we can feel God close by.

Believing in God is not a matter of accepting an abstract idea. Believing in God means gathering in the moments when God feels close by and taking these moments seriously. It means remembering these moments, cherishing them, and saving them. It means pursuing them. And it means learning from them.

How do we find such important moments? If we want a moment with Mom or Dad, we know how to find them. If we want a moment with a teacher, we might go up after class. How do we get a moment with God?

Over the generations of Jewish history, many Jews have had moments when they felt God was close. Because these moments were so important, they wanted to share them with us. So they left behind a trail for us to follow. The trail is marked by a special line of words you might already know:

בָּרוּךְ אַתָּה יְיָ אֱלֹהֵינוּ מֶלֶךְ הָעוֹלָם.

Baruch Ata Adonai, Elohaynu melech ha-olam.
Praised are You, God, Ruler of the Universe.

What we call a "*bracha*"—a blessing—is more than a prayer. It is a trail marker showing us the way to find a moment with God. What comes next in the *bracha* is most important—the description of a moment with God. For example:

בָּרוּךְ אַתָּה יְיָ אֱלֹהֵינוּ מֶלֶךְ הָעוֹלָם
הַמּוֹצִיא לֶחֶם מִן הָאָרֶץ.

Baruch Ata Adonai, Elohaynu melech ha-olam,
ha-motzee lechem min ha-aretz.

Praised are You, God, Ruler of the Universe,

who brings bread from the earth.

Even something regular and boring, like eating my sandwich for lunch, can become a moment when I can feel God is close.

Feeding the world, this *bracha* tells us, is something God does. But it is also something we can do. We can grow food. We can prepare a meal. We can feed hungry people. And when we do that, we are sharing with God the work of feeding people, and we feel God is close.

Near our synagogue, there is a shelter for homeless families. Several times a year, kids from our synagogue youth group go there to prepare and serve meals. I once asked the kids what it feels like to share a meal with people who have nothing and who have known only hunger and want. One kid answered, "I held a serving spoon, and God held my hand."

How do we find moments with God like that one? We look at the *brachot*, the blessings, and follow the path:

בָּרוּךְ אַתָּה יְיָ אֱלֹהֵינוּ מֶלֶךְ הָעוֹלָם
פּוֹקֵחַ עִוְרִים;
מַלְבִּישׁ עֲרוּמִים;
מַתִּיר אֲסוּרִים.

Baruch Ata Adonai, Elohaynu melech ha-olam,

pokeach eev'reem;

malbeesh arumeem;

mateer asureem.

Praised are You, God, Ruler of the Universe,

who helps the blind see;

who gives clothing to the naked;

who frees those who are confined.

These are moments with God that are waiting for you. Could you do any of these things?

I believe that God is real. But God isn't far off in heaven; God is right here. How do we know God is near? By feeling the caring presence of others, of people like Charles. And by feeling our own power to care and to help. We can be God's hands, God's eyes, and God's ears in the world. We can bring God close to others when they are in need, just as others bring God close to us.

Ultimately, the bigger question isn't, "Should I believe in God?" but rather, "What difference does it make?" What difference does it make if there is God? I don't think the point is just to say that God exists, and then go on living as before. The point is to be like God, to live a Godly life. The point is to be a person like Charles and do the caring that God needs done in the world. Because when we care, God is real and close.

3

Do I Have to Go to Services? What Good Is Praying?

"I have to go to services on Saturday for my friend's Bar Mitzvah," reported Daniel to the class. "I hate services. They're sooooo boring." Daniel was being honest. Then, he suddenly remembered that I'm the rabbi, so he retreated. "You go to services every Saturday. Don't you find it boring?"

"No, actually, I like praying," I told him.

This, he couldn't believe. "You actually like it? Why? What good is praying? Does God listen? Does God answer you?"

Abraham Joshua Heschel was an important rabbi and philosopher who lived in the middle of the twentieth century. Heschel traveled around the world, teaching in synagogues, churches, and universities. Whenever he gave an evening lecture, he would begin by telling the audience, "Ladies and gentlemen, a great miracle just happened!" People would stop to listen very carefully, wondering: What miracle happened? Why didn't we see it? Then Heschel would continue, "A great miracle just happened: The sun went down!" Some people would laugh. Some would shake their heads at this crazy rabbi. Others remained puzzled about what he meant. Then Heschel would begin to talk about how a religious person sees the world.

Miracles happen all the time, Heschel taught. Amazing things, magnificent things are happening all around us. But most of us don't notice. We have learned how to ignore them.

We normally think that miracles are events that break the laws of nature—seas that split, plagues that fall from the sky, or sticks that turn into snakes. Heschel understood that the most remarkable things are not these rare and unusual events, but the normal, regular, everyday things that we never notice. How can normal things be miracles? It's all in how we look at them.

Have you ever been really sick? Do you remember how wonderful it felt when you started to get better? Do you remember when the fever went away, or the first time that you could swallow without pain? It's an amazing feeling. Maybe you promised yourself that you'd never forget how great it feels. You promised that you'd appreciate your health and never take being healthy for granted again! That lasted about thirty minutes, and then you forgot; we all do. What could be more wonderful than being healthy—feeling all the parts of your body working well? Being healthy is a miracle, but one that most of us never notice. Yet how much happier would we be if we could just notice each day how wonderful it is to be healthy? We would probably complain a lot less about small things that bother and annoy us if we looked upon our health as a precious gift. And we might take better care of ourselves.

The religious person, taught Heschel, notices the miracles. The religious person notices how amazing things—all things—really are. The religious person stops and wonders at the beauty of a sunset, the power of a thunderstorm, and the kindness of a stranger. The opposite of being religious, according to Heschel, isn't a person who doesn't believe in God, but a person who doesn't notice all the amazing things around us. The opposite of being religious is being bored.

We've discussed the moments we have when we feel God close to us. Heschel believed that these moments can happen all the time. The problem is that we're distracted. We're too busy. We have homework to complete and piano to practice. We have TV shows to watch and phone calls to make. We have places to go and things to do. We are very busy people. And we miss the opportunities to feel God close by.

Prayer is a way to learn how to stop and notice the miracles around us. Prayer is a way to have a moment with

God. Most people think that prayer is a way of asking for things from God, but only a very little bit of Jewish prayer is "asking prayer." Most Jewish prayers get us to stop and notice. Prayer in Judaism is a way to learn mindfulness—how to pay attention to the miracles that are all around us.

How do you wake up in the morning? I'm not what you'd call a "morning person." I wake up with a grumble and a groan. I'm usually late, so there's a rush to the bathroom, to breakfast, and then out the door to work. Never do I notice the miracle of a new day—a new chance at living, a new chance at learning, a new chance to find friendship. So I've learned to force myself to stop for just a few seconds and say a prayer:

מוֹדֶה אֲנִי לְפָנֶיךָ, מֶלֶךְ חַי וְקַיָּם,
שֶׁהֶחֱזַרְתָּ בִּי נִשְׁמָתִי בְּחֶמְלָה; רַבָּה אֱמוּנָתֶךָ.

Modeh ani lefanecha melech chai v'kayam sheh-hech-
ezar-ta bee nishmatee bichemla raba emoonatecha.
Thank you God, Source of Life, for the gifts of
life and energy and this new day.

Take ten seconds each morning to stop and say thank you for the miracle of this new day. Take ten seconds to think about what's possible in this new day and what you could do with this day.

The purpose of prayer is not to change God. The purpose of prayer is to change us. The purpose of prayer is to make us aware of the miracles around us and the moments of God's closeness waiting for us each day. Prayer doesn't bring heaven down; prayer brings us up. So the question in the end is not, Does God hear my prayers? Rather, ask: Do I hear my prayers? Am I listening? Am I paying attention? Do I notice the miracles happening around me all the time?

IF I PRAY FOR SOMETHING, WILL I GET IT?

Daniel wasn't satisfied.

"On Hanukkah, I asked God for a certain toy. I didn't get it. Did God forget about me? If I pray for something, will I get it? Does God answer that kind of prayer?"

Suppose you have a test in a class you don't like, so you don't bother to study. (You'd rather watch TV.) A few minutes before the test, you begin praying, "Please God, help me on this test!" Will it help? Three days later, the teacher passes back your test. She puts the paper face down on your desk. You're scared to look at the grade. So, you pray again, "Please God, let it be a good grade!" Will it help?

In the Talmud, there's an important teaching:

A woman is pregnant and about to give birth. Her husband wants a son, so he prays, "Please God, let it be a boy!" This is an empty prayer. A man coming home from a trip hears a fire alarm in his town. He prays, "Please God, not my house!" This is empty prayer (*Mishna Brachot* 9:3).

Jewish tradition believes in the power of prayer—but only intelligent prayer. There are intelligent prayers, and there are empty prayers. Why are these prayers empty?

The father who prays for a son is asking God to change something that's already been determined. God doesn't work that way. That's an empty prayer.

The person who prays that the emergency be at someone else's house is asking God to change something that's already been determined—and more, he's asking that something bad be put on someone else. That's *really* empty prayer.

There is a difference between prayer and magic. A magician pretends to use his powers to change things in the world just by saying magic words. The most famous magic words are actually an old Hebrew spell: *Abra-Kadabra* is Hebrew for "I will make it as I say it."

We know that magic is not real. Rabbits don't come out of hats. And the lady isn't really cut in two and then reattached. It's pretend.

Expecting God to change the world just because you want it changed is also magic. And like magic, it's not real. It doesn't happen. God doesn't work that way. That's empty prayer.

So you didn't study for the test and you got a bad grade. But this issue of empty prayer can be much more serious: A mom and dad once came to talk with me. They were very upset because their daughter had been diagnosed with a terrible disease. They prayed and prayed, but the daughter's condition only got worse. They asked me, "Why doesn't God answer our prayers and make her better?" They figured that God must have some reason to ignore their prayers, and that reason must have something to do with them. They imagined that they had done something wrong and that God was punishing them. "What did we do to deserve this? Why is God so mad at us?" they asked me through their tears.

I felt so bad for these people—they were really hurting. First, they hurt because their child was sick. Second, they hurt more by believing that God refused to hear their prayers because of something they had done. They ended up believing that they had brought pain on their child, which is the worst pain a parent can feel. Third, they hurt even more because they couldn't figure out what they had done that was so bad to deserve such a punishment and what they could do about it. Sometimes even just an idea can really hurt.

Real prayer, prayer that works, I explained to them, doesn't change the world; it changes us. We can't ask God to change the world for us. We have to do that for ourselves. We can only ask God for the wisdom, strength, and courage to change it ourselves. When I was sick with cancer, I told them, I didn't pray for the cancer to go away. I knew that was an empty prayer. I prayed, instead, for the courage to keep hoping and not give up. I prayed for the strength to take the medicine, even though it was awful. I prayed that my family wouldn't worry too much. I asked God for the wisdom to help me live well in whatever amount of time I had left. And God answered my prayers.

They were still very worried about their daughter. She was in pain, and they were in pain. But they stopped believing God was punishing them. They stopped imagining they had done something wrong. So we held hands and we prayed together. We asked God to give us the wisdom to take good care of their little girl. We prayed for the strength and courage to get through this terrible time with hope and love for one another. We prayed that she would know how much she is loved. And I think God answered their prayers, too.

Do I Have to Go to a Synagogue to Pray?

"All right," Daniel conceded, "so praying is cool. But do I have to go to synagogue to pray? Why can't I just go into the woods or out to the beach and talk with God?"

You *can* go into the woods or out to the beach and talk with God. In fact, some of the best moments of prayer I've ever had were out in nature, far away from synagogues and services. You can go anywhere to pray.

The synagogue gives us a different experience of prayer. It is the experience of a community sharing prayer together and living life together.

Did you ever go to a baseball or football game? What's the difference between watching the game at the ballpark and watching the same game at home on TV? Unless you have really good seats, you probably see more on TV than from your seat in the ballpark. So why is the ballpark always a better experience? Because there's more than just the game going on. There's the game. And there's the crowd and their cheers, doing "the wave," screaming for the home team, and screaming at the other guys. There's the popcorn and the peanuts, the funny hats, those big foam fingers. It's the whole scene.

A synagogue service is to prayer what the afternoon at the ballpark is to the ball game. We pray, but we pray together. We blend our voices together in song. We share our lives with one another—happy moments and celebrations, as well as sad moments, tragedies, and the losses that come with life. We learn together—sharing our ideas about how life should be lived. When life is good, we share the joy. When life is difficult, we help one another find the courage not to give up, not to lose hope.

In the woods, I feel the presence of God in the peacefulness of the trees. At the beach, I feel the presence of God in the rhythm of the waves and the vastness of the ocean. In synagogue, I feel the presence of God in the sounds of all of us who have gathered to celebrate life together. In synagogue, I know that I belong—that my life matters to all these people. I am touched by the lives of others, and they are touched by me.

4

Talking Snakes and Splitting Seas ... Is Any of That Stuff in the Bible True?

Jennifer came to class early one afternoon. "I just had my first Bat Mitzvah lesson. I have to learn a whole section of the Torah, and then I have to talk about it in front of everybody!" she said nervously. "Rabbi, do you really believe in all these stories? Does anyone? Are the stories in the Bible true?"

On the fourth Thursday in November, people in the United States gather together with their families and friends for a special feast. We eat turkey, stuffing, cranberry sauce, sweet potatoes, corn bread, and pumpkin pie. Before we eat all these wonderful foods, we tell a story. The story goes something like this:

In the year 1620, our Pilgrim ancestors left England, where they were persecuted, to find freedom in America. They sailed across the Atlantic Ocean on a ship called the *Mayflower* and landed in a cold, forbidding place: Massachusetts. Unfamiliar with their surroundings, the

Pilgrims starved. They would all have died had not the natives of that place come to help them. The natives taught the Pilgrims to grow local crops and hunt for game. With their help, the Pilgrims survived their first year and prospered in that place. After the next year's harvest, the Pilgrims held a feast to express gratitude to the natives for their help and to God for the gifts of survival and prosperity. And so we gather each year at this holiday of Thanksgiving to express our gratitude for the gifts of our lives.

We all know this story. But is it true?

Parts of it are true. The Pilgrims did come to America in 1620 on a ship called the *Mayflower*. They did settle in Plymouth, Massachusetts. They did have a tough time of it. And the natives did help them.

Parts of the story, on the other hand, aren't exactly fact.

For one thing, *my* ancestors weren't in Massachusetts in 1620. They were still in Eastern Europe. How can I talk about "my Pilgrim ancestors"?

For another, while the Pilgrims might have held a feast to thank the natives for their help, after dinner they pushed the natives aside and stole the continent from them! That part is somehow left out of our telling of the story.

Even if all the *facts* of the story aren't true, the *story* is still true. Because more than any other, this story tells us what it means to be an American.

To be an American is to tell this story in the first person—to say "my Pilgrim ancestors"—no matter where you came from and when you got here. Because all of us came here for the same reason: We were escaping from persecution and tyranny, looking for freedom.

Whether your ancestors landed at Plymouth, Massachusetts, Ellis Island in New York City, or San Francisco Bay, moving here was tough. Starting over in a new place takes tremendous courage. But somehow, we made it. And now we enjoy a special kind of life that is unique among the peoples of the world. Whatever our faith or religion, we understand the importance of taking a few moments each year to express gratitude for the gifts of America and for the privilege of living in this great land.

The most important part of the story is what our ancestors called themselves. They weren't the Refugees, or Immigrants, or Aliens, or Strangers. They called themselves Pilgrims. A pilgrim is someone who takes a journey to a special, sacred place. The story teaches us to look for what's special and sacred in America. That's what makes it a true story. We can understand Bible stories the same way. Bible stories are true, even if all the facts aren't accurate. Was there a Noah who built a boat and saved animals from a flood? We don't know. But the story is true: It teaches us that people can mess up the world by the choices they make, and people can save the world by the choices they make.

The Bible uses stories to teach us the most important truths of our lives.

Did all humanity come from one couple, Adam and Eve? Again, we don't know. But the story is true because it teaches us something very powerful: All human beings are one family. Therefore, all human beings are responsible for one another. People of other faiths, people with skin of a different color, people who live in other parts of the city or the nation or on the other side of the planet, people different from "us"—we are all part of the same family, and we are all responsible for one another.

It might be interesting to find out if the stories happened the way the Bible says they did. But the truth of a story is not in what happened a long time ago in a place far away. A story's truth is what it tells us about our lives right now. Can we find ourselves in the story?

Did a snake really convince Eve to eat the forbidden fruit? Personally, I haven't met many talking snakes. But I do know what it's like to be tempted to do something that I know is wrong. I know what that voice sounds like—and how hard it is to resist! What do you do when you hear that voice?

Was there a Moses who freed the Israelites from slavery? Did the ten plagues happen as the Torah tells us? Did the Red Sea really split?

If the story of the Pilgrims tells us what it means to be an American, the Passover story tells us what it means to be Jewish.

To be Jewish is to remember Egypt and all the other times in our history when we were slaves. What does it mean to be a slave? It means that we were treated not as people, not even as living creatures, but as objects. A slave is a person turned into a thing. We remember that, and we promise never to treat people that way; never to let any-one, anywhere be treated as a thing. We dream of a world where all people are treated as God's special creations. And we devote ourselves to making that dream come true. The ethics of the Jewish religion provide a way of making that dream come true.

To be Jewish is to remember what happened to Pharaoh. He thought he was a god and commanded people to worship him. In the end, however, his stubborn arrogance destroyed him.

To be Jewish is to remember Moses. One man, speaking the truth, was able to change history and free his people.

To be Jewish is to never give up hope. No matter how powerful evil may be, it can never destroy our dreams; it cannot enslave our imagination, our spirit, or our love. The Red Sea split. One day, all evil will drown itself and we will find ourselves on the road to the Promised Land.

The Bible tells us the most important truths about being alive. That's what makes it true.

IF GOD TALKED TO EVERYONE IN THE BIBLE, WHY DOESN'T GOD TALK TO ANYONE TODAY?

By now, the whole class had arrived, and everyone joined in Jennifer's discussion of Bible stories. Billy, who was still searching for a way to believe in God, asked, "If God talked to everyone in the Bible, why doesn't God talk to anyone today?"

The Talmud, the great sourcebook of Judaism, was put together about 1,500 years ago. There is a story in the Talmud that I really love about the great Rabbis who lived in the second century:

> The Rabbis were debating about a certain kind of oven. One of the greatest of the Rabbis, Rabbi Eliezer, gave every reason that the oven should be used. But the other Rabbis disagreed. Rabbi Eliezer wanted so badly to prove that he was right, he brought all kinds of miracles as proof. He made trees dance. He made a stream of water flow backward. He even made the walls of the academy start to fall over. The other Rabbis admired his ability to make miracles, but they answered, "In our discussion, miracles don't count as proof."
>
> Finally, Rabbi Eliezer said, "If I'm right, let God prove it!" And then, the Talmud tells us, the voice of God was heard to say: "Rabbi Eliezer is right! Why are you arguing with Rabbi Eliezer? He's always right!"
>
> At that moment, another great Rabbi, Rabbi Joshua, arose and responded: "The Torah is not in heaven!" (Bava Metzia 59b).

Rabbi Joshua was actually quoting the Torah. In Deuteronomy, Moses says to the People Israel, shortly before his death:

> This commandment I've given you today is not too difficult for you, nor is it far away. It is not in heaven, that you should say: "Who among us can go to the heavens and get it for us and give it to us that we may do it?" Neither is it beyond the sea, that you should say, "Who among us can cross to the other side of the sea and get it for us and teach it to us that we may do it?" No, it is very close to you, in your mouth and in your heart, to do it (Deuteronomy 30:11–14).

What did Rabbi Joshua mean by this? God gave us the Torah. And God gave us the responsibility to understand it and teach it. But if God were to show up every time we try and tell us we're wrong, we'll never get to do it ourselves. If God shows up each time, we'll never learn responsibility. To fulfill God's wish that we become responsible, God has to let us make our own decisions. In other words, Rabbi Joshua told God to back off!

There's a wonderful ending to this story. Some time later, there lived a rabbi, Rabbi Nathan, who was visited from time to time by the prophet Elijah. According to the Bible, Elijah never died; he was taken into heaven in a fiery chariot (II Kings 2:11–12). In the imagination of the Rabbis,

Elijah lives forever, going around the world doing special things for special people and showing up at our seder tables each Pesach. When they met, Rabbi Nathan asked Elijah, "What did God do when Rabbi Joshua told God to back off?" Elijah answered, "He laughed with joy and said, 'My children have defeated me! My children have defeated me!'"

At some point, every mother and father has to back off and let kids do it their way (as long as they don't hurt themselves), even if they make mistakes. Otherwise, kids will never grow up and become responsible. There is a time for parents to tell kids what to do, and there's a time for parents to let kids assume responsibility.

If God keeps giving directions, we will never grow up. There is a time for God to speak, and there is a time for God to trust us to understand and be responsible.

God still speaks to us today. Not directly, but through the words of the Torah and the Prophets, the wisdom of the tradition, the symbols and rituals of our religion. When we think hard to understand the meaning of Torah and tradition, that's God's voice speaking through us. When we work hard making the dreams and ideals of the tradition part of our lives, that's God's voice showing us the way. When we teach others the wisdom of our tradition, that's God's voice teaching. Our sense of responsibility to God and to the Torah is an echo of the voice of God.

5

Why Does God Let Terrible Things Happen?

One afternoon at recess time everyone went outside for some fresh air, a snack, and a quick game of soccer—everyone except Molly. She just sat at her place looking dreamily out the window.

"Molly, are you OK?" I asked.

"I'm just depressed," she responded.

"Something going on? Anything I can do to help?"

"My aunt has cancer. She's probably going to die. My mom has been crying all week. And I don't know what to do or say to make her feel better." And Molly began to cry.

"Rabbi, sometimes life can be so hard. Why does God let such bad things happen?"

One Monday morning in January 1994, a powerful earthquake hit the northern sections of Los Angeles, where we lived. Our home was destroyed. It felt like the whole house went over a speed bump. Every window was shattered. Every wall crumbled. All our furniture fell over and most of our belongings were smashed. By some miracle, no one was hurt.

Some days later, the insurance company sent an inspector to look over the damage. He spent hours looking over the ruins of my house, and then he sat down to talk to us about our things. In the course of the conversation, he asked me what I did for a living. I told him I was a rabbi. He shook his head, "For a rabbi, your house sure took a beating! I thought God was supposed to take care of people like you!"

"God did take care of us," I answered. "He sent you!"

There are people who believe that everything that happens to them is God's decision. Everything, they believe, happens for a reason, even if only God knows the reason. If something good happens, they thank God. If something bad happens, they feel better thinking it was no accident. God brought this to them; therefore, it must be for the best. When bad things happen, they conclude that God is punishing them. All they need to do is figure out what they did wrong.

But if something really terrible happens, they might get angry and scream at God or give up on God. After all, they reason, if God is supposed to take care of them, how could this happen? What could they have done to deserve this? Like the family we talked about before, these poor people suffer three times as much: They suffer the bad things that have happened to them. And then they suffer double because they believe that they did something to deserve it; they think they're being punished. And they suffer triple because most of the time, they can't figure out what they did to deserve it. They feel guilt, they feel hurt, and they feel God has abandoned them.

I don't agree with this way of thinking about God. I don't believe that God decides everything that happens to us. I don't believe that God punishes us with earthquakes and diseases and accidents. I don't believe, for example, that God sent the earthquake to destroy my house, or that God sends diseases that destroy the lives of our loved ones.

In the Talmud there is a discussion of this question:

> Suppose a man stole a bag of seeds and planted them in his garden. What would happen? It would be right if the seeds didn't grow! But nature follows its own rules, and the seeds grow. Suppose a man had relations with his neighbor's wife. It would be right if she did not get pregnant. But nature follows its own rules, and she gets pregnant (*Avoda Zara* 54b).

Nature follows its own rules, and God doesn't stop it. God doesn't break nature's rules.

According to nature's rules, the earth's crust moves, and that causes earthquakes. It wasn't God's decision that made the earth shake and wreck all the houses on my street. And God didn't break nature's rule just because a rabbi lived on the block. My house was wrecked, too.

So, where was God?

Some amazing things happened in the days following the earthquake. Right after the shaking stopped, there was a loud knock at my door. It was my neighbors, checking to make sure everyone was safe. They were afraid we were hurt or trapped and brought tools, lanterns, and first aid.

For three days following the quake, we stayed in the wrecked shell of our house to pack our things and get ready to move. During that time there was no water, no gas, and no electricity. We had to buy bottled water, but everywhere we went to get it, the price was doubled or tripled. One afternoon, a big yellow truck pulled onto our block. A guy and his son were selling water—for even less than the regular price. When I asked him why, he explained that he lived in another town that was unaffected by the quake. He saw the terrible damage on the TV news and wanted to help, so he and his young son rented this truck, bought all the bottled water they could find, and brought it out to us. He was just glad he could help. He was glad he could show his son how to help. Where was God in the earthquake? Maybe God was in the strong hands of my neighbors, or in the kind generosity of the man in the yellow truck.

God isn't the cause of tragedy. Tragedy happens because we live in nature, and nature includes earthquakes and diseases. You can find God in our courage to get through and in our willingness to share kindness and support to survive the tragedy.

How Can Anyone Believe in God
after the Holocaust?

*Recess was over, and everyone came in to join our
discussion.*

"We've been reading The Diary of Anne Frank *in
my English class," Jennifer related. "I just keep thinking
about how unfair it is that she was killed in the concentration camp and never got to grow up."*

*"My grandma was in the Holocaust," reported Daniel.
"She has these numbers on her arm. But she never talks
about it."*

*"Rabbi," asked Molly, "what about the Holocaust?
How can anyone believe in God after the Holocaust?"*

The Holocaust is the worst tragedy in all of human history.
The evil of the Holocaust is so horrible that there are no
words to describe it. Saying "6 million Jews were murdered"
or "11 million innocent people died" cannot begin to con-
vey how terrible this was. If every individual human life
is precious and irreplaceable, how can one even imagine
6 million or 11 million?

How do we find God after a tragedy as huge as
the Holocaust? This may be the hardest question for any
religious person today.

One who believes that God decides what happens
to every human being cannot answer this question. How
could there be a reason for the destruction of 6 million Jews,

including 1 million Jewish children? It's no wonder that many people stopped believing in God after the Holocaust.

Remember the Talmud's teaching. God doesn't stop nature from following its own rules. Human beings have a nature. The most important part of human nature is our ability to make choices. We can choose to be good or evil, to do good or evil. We choose to be loving or hateful, to build or to destroy. And just as God doesn't interfere when nature follows its own rules, God doesn't stop human beings from making their own choices. Even when they choose the worst of evil.

Human beings chose to build the concentration camps and the gas chambers and to murder millions. That was a human choice, not God's decision.

But God was not entirely absent from the Holocaust. God didn't check out. Just as in the earthquake, God was present wherever human beings found the ability to resist the evil, to overcome the pain, to share kindness and care, and to get through the tragedy.

I'm sure you've heard of Hitler. You may even know the names of Himmler, Goering, and Goebbels. These were the leaders of the Nazis. But have you ever heard of Joop Westerweel, Sempo Sugihara, and Raul Wallenberg? Do you know who they were?

The Nazis enlisted thousands of people to help them murder the Jews of Europe. Millions of others stood by and ignored it all and let it happen. (After the war they claimed, "We didn't know what was going on.") But there were others, very few, who resisted. They were not Jewish, but they risked their lives to save Jews from the Nazis.

Joop Westerweel was a Dutch teacher who organized an "underground railroad," leading small groups of Jews by bicycle out of Holland, all the way across France, and into Spain, a neutral country where Jews were safe. He saved dozens of Jews. In 1944, he was caught by the Nazis. They killed him for saving Jewish lives.

Sempo Sugihara was a Japanese ambassador stationed in Lithuania. When the Nazis invaded that country, the Jews were trapped. The Nazis were on one side eager to kill them. On the other side were the Russians, who wouldn't let them in. Russia would open its border and let the Jews in only if they had special visas—like passports—showing that they were on their way to somewhere else. But no country would give them these visas. Finally, in desperation, the Jews came to Sugihara and begged him for help. Sugihara's superiors in Tokyo told him not to help the Jews, but he ignored that order. He saw the fear in the eyes of these Jews and he knew that he had to help. Sugihara began writing visas for Jews. With the help of his wife and son, Sugihara wrote 3,500 visas in one night, saving more than 10,000 Jewish lives.

Raul Wallenberg was a diplomat from Sweden assigned to the Swedish embassy in Budapest, Hungary. He was shocked at what the Nazis were doing to Jews. He set up a special zone in Budapest, under the direction of the Red Cross, where Jews were safe from the Nazis. Wallenberg worked tirelessly bringing Jews to safety, sometimes even pulling them off the trains that would have taken them to the concentration camps. By the end of the war, Wallenberg had saved 30,000 Jews. At the war's end, he disappeared. It is believed that he was arrested by the Soviets and died in a Soviet prison.

Westerweel, Sugihara, and Wallenberg were not Jewish. But they risked their lives—some even gave up their lives—to save Jews from the Nazis. And they were not alone. In every country where the Nazis tried to kill Jews, there were people who risked their own lives to save Jewish lives. These were just ordinary people—farmers, fishermen, Catholic priests and Protestant ministers, teachers, and government officials—who did the right thing. Compared to the thousands who helped the Nazis or the millions who watched and did nothing, these heroes were very few in number, maybe a few thousand. But because of them, we can believe that God was still alive even in the most terrible of places at the most terrible of times.

Bad things happen to us because nature treats us all the same. The earth shakes, and all our homes are destroyed. Our bodies fail, and we get sick. Bad things happen to us because human beings choose to do evil. Sometimes entire nations choose evil, and a Holocaust destroys millions of innocent lives. Bad things happen, but God didn't make them happen. God doesn't punish us in that way.

That doesn't mean that God is absent. Even in the very worst of circumstances, God is present in our ability to overcome and survive, in our ability to share caring and help. God is present in our ability to transform the world—bringing kindness where there was hate, bringing healing where there was pain, bringing hope where there was despair. When we witness tragedy and pain, the real question isn't, Where was God? The real question is, Where are you? What is your response or responsibility if people suffer and the world is ugly?

There is an old story:

A man goes up to heaven at the end of his life. He stands before the throne of God. The man looks up at God and says, "You know, I'm very angry at You! Can't You see that the world You created is filled with suffering and ugliness and destruction? Why don't You do something to fix the world's mess?"

God looks down at the man, and in a gentle voice says, "I did do something. I sent you."

6

What Is God Anyway?

Josh knew sports. In the world of sports, he was a genius. He could cite from memory statistics, records, and the important moments of championship games. When anything else was discussed, he checked out, preferring to sketch sports heroes to participating in our discussions. So it came as a complete surprise one afternoon when his hand went up and, with all the confidence of a boxing champ, he entered the ring.

"We've been talking about God. God, God, God. I still don't believe in God!"

"That's OK. I'm glad to see you're thinking about it," I responded. "Tell me something, what do you mean by the word 'God'?"

He didn't expect this response. "What do you mean, what do I mean by 'God'? You're a rabbi; you know what God is!"

"Well, you've told me you're not sure about God. I just want to be sure I understand what you don't believe. What do you mean by the word 'God'?"

Josh tried to answer. "Most people would say that God is an invisible spirit who lives in heaven and rewards good people and punishes evil people. I just can't believe in that."

He looked at me the way you look at a teacher to see if you got the right answer on the quiz.

"Josh, it's not God you don't believe in," I told him. "It's Santa Claus. Santa Claus brings presents to the good kids and coal to the bad ones. Your problem isn't with God. Because if that's what God is supposed to be, then I don't believe in God, either."

Now he was the one who was shocked. "But you're the rabbi. You've got to believe!"

"Don't I get to believe in something that makes sense to me?" I replied.

When I was a child, I believed that God was a grandfatherly fellow who lived invisibly in heaven and took care of me. I suspect that many people start out with this same idea. As I got older, my ideas about God changed. As we grow more sophisticated, it's important that our ideas of God do also. Otherwise, we get stuck with childish ideas of God and religion that don't fit us any more than the clothes and shoes we wore as little kids. Searching, questioning, debating, trying out different ideas about God is the way we grow religiously.

Here is a way to think about God. When you look at yourself in a mirror, what do you see? You see yourself, right? You see your face, your arms, your shoulders, and your chest. If it's a big mirror, maybe you see your legs and feet. You see your body. But is that you? Is it all of you? Where's your personality? Your sense of humor? The things you know? Your interests and abilities? Can you see that in the mirror?

What's missing from the mirror image? You see your body, but you don't see that part of you we call your "self." And no matter how good-looking you are, your "self" part is much more important! It's the part that makes you ... you! Lots of people have arms and legs. But only you have this "self."

But what is this "self"? What's it made of? Where is it? How did it get here? Isn't it strange that the "self," which is the essence of you, is so hard to describe? It's so close, but it's hard to find words to define it.

Suppose we look at the world in the same way. Imagine the universe—the earth, the stars and planets, all of nature, everything that is, was, and ever will be—like a body. Is there a "self" living in this body?

God is the "self" of the universe.

Just as it is impossible to describe and define your own "self," it is impossible to describe and define God.

In the Torah, God has a personal name. In Hebrew this name is spelled *Yud-Hay-Vav-Hay*. When we see this name, we say "Adonai," which means "my master." But the name itself can't be pronounced. Why a name you can't say? You can only name things that can be defined or described. If you can't define it or describe it, it is difficult to name it. The fuzzier the definition, the fuzzier its name becomes. God, the "self" of the universe, can't be defined. So God's name can't be pronounced.

Even though we can't define God, there are things we can say. We can say what difference it makes to us knowing that God is in the universe.

Look into the mirror again. You've got arms, legs, hair, feet. Each part is different, but they are all one person because they are all part of your "self." The floor you're standing on, the clothes you're wearing, and your shoes aren't part of your "self." It's this sense of "self" that makes your parts into one person. Similarly, to say that the universe has a "self" is to say that everything is *one*. And so we say the *Shema*, the most important prayer in Jewish religion: Hear O Israel, Adonai is God, Adonai is One. The important word is the last word: *One*.

When we're talking about God, we're not talking about someone being up there in heaven, somebody separate from us and from the world, looking down on us. God isn't "up there," or even "out there." God is the All. God is everything. God is what connects everything to everything else. Including us, the ones looking for God.

When we say the *Shema*, our most important prayer, we are saying that God—the All—is not broken up into two, or three, or more. The world can't be divided. You can't say, "This is my place and this is yours," or "These are our people and those are others." You can't divide humanity into "us" and "them." We're all one. We're all connected. If I hurt you, I hurt myself. So Torah commands me to love my neighbor as myself (Leviticus 19:18). My neighbor and me, we're really one.

Imagine a wave on the ocean. Now imagine that God is the ocean and each of us is a wave. A wave is part of the ocean. A wave rises up out of the ocean to become distinct, and then it goes back again. Now, suppose the wave became aware of itself. It might think it was a separate, independent being. What would it take to make the wave discover that it was part of the ocean? And then how would it feel? How would that discovery change the wave's idea of itself? The wave would know that in reality, it was connected to every other wave. It would know that after it had risen and then fallen back into the sea, it wasn't really gone but would rise again as another wave. It would understand that in reality, it was much, much bigger than just one wave.

What difference does this idea of God make in real life?

Most people behave as if they were astronauts. Like astronauts, they think they live in a sealed suit, in a sealed capsule, isolated and insulated from the environment around them. Their space suit is their skin, and inside is what they call "me." When we say we feel close to God, we are recognizing the truth that we're not astronauts. We're not isolated beings. We are part of our environment, part of our community, part of our world. And it's all part of us. Because we're all part of God and God is One.

The problem is, we constantly forget this truth. We forget and we start to think and behave like astronauts, as if nothing we do affects anyone else or the world around us. The most important purpose of religion is to remind us constantly that we are part of the All. That's how our belief in God leads directly to a sense of being responsible for the world.

WHAT'S THAT ABOUT GOD BEING A SHEPHERD ... ARE WE SUPPOSED TO BE SHEEP?

"OK, Rabbi," Josh continued, "but there's this line in the prayer book about God being a shepherd. What's that about? Are we supposed to be sheep? Baaaaa!"

Think again about your "self." What is it? Is it a thing? If we took you apart, piece by piece, we'd find your heart, your lungs, your brain. Would we find your "self"? The self isn't a thing that we touch and look at. If I want to know your "self," or if you want to know mine, how can we do that? I get to know you by listening to what you say. I watch how you act. From the things you do and say I get a sense of what's important to you. Soon I can say that I know you. Every one of us has a unique pattern of behaving that identifies us. If you were to start behaving strangely, we might say, "You're not yourself today." Your unique pattern of behavior is your "self." Self is not a thing, but a pattern of action. With God it works the same way.

In the Torah, Moses asks God our question. He says, "Let me see Your presence." And God responds: "I will make all my goodness pass before you, and I will proclaim before you the name of the Lord, and the grace I will grant and the compassion I will show, but you cannot see my face, for man may not see me and live" (Exodus 33:17–20). Moses is God's closest friend. He wants to know what we want to know: What is God? God tells him, You can't know that. What you can know is what I do in the world, how I love the world and care for the world. Moses accepts this because he understands that knowing God is not a matter of knowing what God is, but what God does.

In the prayer book, we find lots of words describing God—Shepherd, Father, King, Rock, Healer, Redeemer. But these aren't meant to be literally true. God isn't really a shepherd herding sheep around. God isn't really a rock. These are metaphors. A metaphor, you will remember from English class, describes something by comparing it to something else. To unlock a metaphor, we need to find the common idea beneath the metaphor and what it refers to.

What does it mean to say, "God is a Shepherd"? Just as a shepherd takes care of the sheep, we have a sense that God takes care of us. God is a Parent. Just as parents love their kids, protect them, and provide for them, we have a sense that God loves us, protects us, and provides for us. God is King. Just as a monarch sets the rules of an empire, we believe that God gives us the rules for living a good life.

Our religion is full of metaphors for God. But notice what these metaphors tell us: They don't tell us what God *is*, they tell us what God *does*. They describe the pattern of God's actions.

Perhaps we should change the way we talk about God. What if we used the word "God" not as a noun, but as a verb or an adverb? Using "God" as a noun is confusing. It makes us think of God as the name of something that we can see and touch. We imagine God as a giant person living up in heaven. Or we describe God in confusing words like "spirit" or "power" or "being."

Perhaps a better way to use the word "God" is as a verb or an adverb, like "God-ing" or "acting Godly." When we say "God," we're not talking about a person or a thing or a being, we're talking about a pattern of events in the world and in our lives, or about a quality of an action or a moment.

If God is a noun, a thing, we keep asking, What is God? or Where is God? But once we start thinking of God as a verb or an adverb, we can ask different questions. With verbs we can ask When and How questions, like When is God? When are we acting Godly? How can we do God in the world?

Our religion is our way of answering these questions. Our religion helps us find the God that's happening all around us. Our religion teaches us what is the Godly pattern of acting in our world, and what is not. Judaism is an invitation to join in acting Godly, in doing God. When we say that we feel close to God, we are saying that we are involved in God, participating in God, living Godly.

When the film *The Prince of Egypt* was being made, I had a friend at the studio who invited me to see an early version of the film and to meet the director. The filmmakers had a problem: When Moses hears God's voice at the burning bush, what does God sound like? Should God sound like Darth Vader? Should God's voice be a man's voice or a woman's voice? A gentle voice or an angry voice? I remembered that this same question was discussed by the ancient Rabbis. The Rabbis came up with an astonishing answer: The voice Moses heard was his own voice. And that's how it turned out in the film! When Moses hears God's voice from the burning bush, it's his own voice commanding him to go and free his people. God's voice doesn't come from far away. If we're part of God, God can speak to us from the deepest part of ourselves. The great problem is learning to listen.

The Bible's very first chapter says that God created the human being "in God's image." What does this mean? Perhaps it teaches that if we want to find God, we need not look up to heaven or out into the universe. The closest place to find God is within each of us. When I pray, I'm not praying "up" to God who lives in heaven. I'm looking deep within myself, trying to find the parts of me that best reflect God.

When I hear God, it's not like the booming voice of a loudspeaker coming from above, but the voice of the deepest part of me pleading for me to live a more Godly life.

When God acts in the world, it's not through thunder-and-lightning miracles from the sky. It's through the selfless acts of people like Charles, who heal and help.

7

What's the Meaning of Life? Is That a Dumb Question?

What's Life For?

Everyone in the class came in very excited.

"You'll never guess who came to school today!" exclaimed
Ashley, *who is our class film, TV, and music critic.*

"Who?" I responded, clueless.

She waited a dramatic second, and then rolled out a
name.

"Who's that?" I asked. Honestly, I'd never heard the
name.

"What universe to do you live in?" asked Ashley, rolling her
eyes with exasperation. "He's just the hottest star of the greatest
show that's ever been on TV. How could you not know?!"

"Is he important?"

"He's gorgeous! He's famous! And he's probably rich.
What else is there?"

"Is *he* important?" I tried again.

"What's important got to do with it? Isn't being rich and famous and beautiful enough for one life? Isn't that what everyone wants?"

"But is it worth wanting? Will it really make you happy?"

Ashley, who has spent a good part of her life studying the lives and loves of celebrities, now begins to reflect. "Rabbi, can I ask you a dumb question? What else is there besides becoming rich and famous? What's life for? What's the meaning of life?"

W hy is this a dumb question? I think it's about the most important question you can ask.

Asking this question means you're taking life seriously. You're asking, What's worth caring about? What's worth worrying about? What's worth working for? What's going to give me the greatest satisfaction? What will make me happiest in life? Would being rich and famous make us happy? Would it give us a life that matters?

Some years ago, someone gave my family a gift: a year's subscription to *People* magazine. At first I laughed at this. What a trashy, gossipy, awful excuse for a magazine. But as I read *People*, I discovered that it has a great wisdom to teach. *People* magazine has pages and pages about rich, famous, and beautiful people ... and how utterly miserable they are. They do drugs. They can't stay married to the same person for more than a few minutes. Their kids hate them.

They have no friends. And they're always worried about losing it all. For all their riches, fame, and beauty, these people aren't happy.

The Talmud has a remarkable teaching:

> "Without bread, there's no Torah. And without
> Torah, there's no bread" (*Pirke Avot* 3:17).

The first part, I understand. People who are starving think about nothing else but their starvation. Torah is the last thing on your mind when you're really hungry.

It's the second part that is really interesting. If you have no Torah—if you have no bigger purpose in life, no idea what life is for—then what good is having tons of money?

The world we live in, according to an old Jewish tradition, is broken. Our world is filled with jagged edges and shattered pieces. We touch the world's brokenness in all the evils we meet in the world—disease, violence, hate, war, hunger, poverty, and ignorance.

The world needs repair. God has invited us to share the work of repairing the world. That's what the Bible means when it says we have a "covenant" with God. We are God's partners. Our job is to repair the world. The world that we meet is a mixture of order and mess, of good and evil, of darkness and light. It is our job, as God's partners, to bring order to the mess, to bring good out of evil, to cast light into the darkness. God needs us. God has a dream of a whole, unbroken, finished world. God needs our help to fulfill that dream.

Imagine being important enough to be God's part-
ner! What a huge honor! What a huge responsibility!

No one has the power to do the whole job alone. You
need help from friends, teachers, and allies. But neither can
you run away from your responsibility. You are needed.

There is a corner of the world that is yours. It is broken, and only you can fix it. It is a mess, and only you can
make it beautiful. You were created with a special blend
of abilities to do this job. You must find that corner and
apply to it all your energies, talents, imagination, and intel-
ligence. That's your mission. That's your purpose. And that's
the meaning of your life.

*"But Rabbi," Ashley tried to persuade me, "he's my hero!
He's a star! He's so famous! Wouldn't it be great to be
famous?"*

Does being famous make you a hero?

Erin Brockovich saved the people of a whole town
from the poison a local factory was dumping in their water.
They made a movie about her life, and Julia Roberts played
her in the movie. A billion or so people saw Julia Roberts win
the Oscar for playing Erin Brockovich. What award did Erin
Brockovich win for saving those people? Everyone knows
what Julia Roberts looks like. She's famous. Does anyone
know what Erin Brockovich looks like? I didn't. I met Erin
Brockovich. I stood on line behind her in the supermarket.
I didn't know who she was until the clerk asked her for her

driver's license when she wrote a check. (I guess he didn't know who she was, either.) Isn't it strange who becomes famous? Given the choice, do you think most people would rather be Erin Brockovich, or Julia Roberts—the person who saved a whole town, or the actor who played her in the movie? Who is the real hero?

I've met heroes in my life.

Jonathan was the smartest kid in my Hebrew School class. After graduating from high school, he went off to a big Ivy League college. We were all really proud of him. A couple of years ago, I found my old friend again. He's a doctor working in research. He could have been very, very rich, but he's made a different choice. He spends all his time searching for the way to cure cancer and AIDS. He's got an army of scientists and researchers working with him in a major university laboratory. If he's successful, he may win a Nobel Prize. But that's not why he works so hard. He just wants to find the cures that will restore life to those who suffer.

Mark was the worst student in Hebrew School. The very, very worst. And his life only went down from there. He became a criminal and a drug addict. Eventually, he ended up in state prison. But something told him he could do more. When he got out of prison, he helped set up a center for kids who were in trouble. He teaches that every person can change his or her life, that each person can lift himself or herself up to a life of goodness. This is what Judaism calls *Teshuva*. Mark is a champion of *Teshuva*. Mark helps kids to get free of drugs and to stay away from crime. He teaches them to live decent, good lives—lives that matter. He has saved hundreds of kids who would have been destroyed by their bad choices.

You couldn't find two men as different as Jonathan and Mark. They are my heroes. Each has found the corner of the world he is uniquely responsible for. And each gives his heart and soul to fixing that corner. Each lives a life that matters. Each has found the meaning of his life. You can, too.

8

No Cheeseburgers?
No Going to the Mall
on Saturday? Why Does
Religion Need So
Many Rules?

Michael arrived with a bag of fast food.

"Michael, I'm sorry," I tell him, "but you can't eat that here. It's the rules."

"What kind of crazy rules?!" He's frustrated. But he gets the question. "Why does religion need to have so many rules? What's God got against cheeseburgers?"

Once, long ago, I joined a gym. Along with my new membership came one session with a trainer. His name was Bobby. Bobby had muscles on his muscles. He looked like he'd spent his life in the gym. Bobby talked to me about all the good things exercise could do for me. He took me through a workout and showed me how to use all the exercise machines in the gym. He taught me how to put together a program that would get me into shape. Then he asked me a very simple question: "How often can you get here?"

He continued, "Can you make it five days a week?"

"I'm pretty busy," I said. "That's going to be hard."

"OK," he said, "four days a week?"

"I don't know," I replied.

"Three days a week?" He was looking worried.

"I'm not sure; my schedule is pretty tight."

"Two days? Once a week?" I shook my head.

"Well," Bobby concluded, "you're not ready to be serious, are you? And if you're not serious," he warned me, "you can't do this right. You can't just wish yourself a new body; you have to do something. You have to do something every single day to make it happen. Come back when you're ready to be serious."

Bobby was right. If I really wanted results, I needed to be serious, which meant putting in some real time in the gym. And that would mean making some real changes in the way I live my life.

Maybe Bobby was a prophet. He asked the question the Torah might ask us: "Are you ready to be serious?" You say you want to be a better person. You say you want to make the world a better place. Doing these things requires changing ourselves and the way we live. That's hard work. It means doing something every day. That's why our religion has so many rules. Like Bobby's exercises, the rules set out the ways we make ourselves better and make our world better every day. But they work only if we're serious.

Let's start with cheeseburgers.

If you read the first chapters of the Bible, you will discover that human beings were supposed to be vegetarians (see Genesis 1:29 and 2:15). In the Garden of Eden, we ate only fruits and vegetables. We lived in peace with nature. Animals didn't fear us, and the world was without conflict and violence. That was God's dream. But humans had other ideas. We wanted to eat meat.

Let's remember something: Eating meat means killing something. We tend to forget this because our meat comes all nicely wrapped from the market or served on a bun with pickles and ketchup at McDonald's. But before it reached the market or the restaurant, that burger was a living, breathing creature that someone had to kill. There's violence involved in the eating of meat.

One ancient Rabbi suggested that anyone who really wants to eat meat should have to kill the animal himself or herself. Think about that. If you really wanted a burger, they'd bring you the animal and a sharp knife, and you'd have to look the animal in the eye and do the killing yourself. Sounds gross? That was the Rabbi's point. If it's disgusting to imagine killing the animal ourselves, why is it less gross if someone else does it for us?

Although God dreamed that we'd be vegetarians, God recognized that people want meat. The laws of *kashrut*, keeping kosher, are God's compromise. Their purpose is to let us kill animals for food but preserve our love and respect for life. Kill animals if you must, but don't become a killer.

Many people make the mistake of thinking that the laws of *kashrut* are intended to keep us healthy. Keeping healthy is also a mitzvah, a commandment of God, but that's not the purpose of *kashrut*. You can eat a very healthy non-kosher diet and a very unhealthy kosher one. The real purpose has to do with the value of life and controlling our power to kill.

If you're a vegetarian, you automatically keep kosher. But if you eat meat or fish, there are four basic laws of *kashrut*:

1. Only certain animals may be eaten. There is nothing really special about the choice of which animals we eat and which we don't. God didn't make pigs and lobsters forbidden because they are more beloved than cows and salmon. Nor are they any cleaner or more holy. The idea is that we're not allowed to go out and just kill whatever we feel like killing. Our killing is limited to a specific list of permitted animals.

2. The animal must be killed in the most painless way possible. Even an animal designated for our food has feeling. You may kill to eat, but you may not allow the animal to suffer.

3. All the blood must be removed from the meat. Blood symbolizes life because blood is always moving in a living body and provides life to the organism. All life belongs to God. You may eat the animal,

but you must not imagine that you created the life of this animal.

4. All foods made from milk and all foods made from meat must be prepared, served, and eaten separately. Meat, which involves killing, symbolizes the taking of life. Milk, which nourishes newborns, symbolizes the giving of life. The two must never be confused in our lives.

In keeping milk and meat separate, we are taught that our real tasks are to limit our desire to destroy life, and to develop our abilities to give life. This is something our culture badly needs to learn. Think about movies, for example. How many movies contain terrible violence—killing people, hurting people, blowing things up—and we just laugh and have a great time? Is there something wrong here? Should violence and death be considered entertainment? Should violence and death be fun to watch?

What's wrong with a cheeseburger? First, we don't know how the animal was killed. Were those who killed the animal careful that the animal didn't suffer? Or did they just kill it the easiest way, even if it hurt the animal? Second, we don't know if they drained out the blood. Most animals we eat were raised on huge ranches and killed in huge factories where no one ever cares that they are living creatures. Finally, cheese, which is made from milk, is mixed up with meat. Life is mixed up with death. Violence is mixed up with pleasure. Saying no to a cheeseburger is a way of saying no to a world that mixes up life and death, violence and fun.

The rules of *kashrut* keep us thinking about the preciousness of life and God's dream of a peaceful world. Every time we pick up a fork and wonder if it is for milk or meat, we are awakened to the ancient dream of a world free of violence.

Michael stuffed his fast-food bag into his desk, but he was ready with another question.

"OK, now I understand the rules about food, but what's this about not going to the mall on Saturday? That's the best day to go to the mall!"

Have you ever seen those stories on TV about the people who won the lottery? One day this guy wakes up, and he's a multimillionaire. Ever wonder how your life would change if you were suddenly a multimillionaire? Suddenly, you wouldn't have to worry about earning a living anymore. You'd have more than enough. You'd be free. You'd work only if you wanted to. You'd get to live on your own terms, do whatever you wanted. So what would you do? Would you continue in school? Would you take a job? Would you do art? Make music? Travel the world?

Do you know what's amazing about those stories of people who win the lottery? It's how unhappy so many of them are. All that money, all the possibilities, all the freedom, and they don't know what to do with it. These are people who have spent their entire lives dreaming of being rich and free. Now they've got it—and it drives them crazy! They don't know how to be free. They don't know what to do with their new freedom.

In the Torah, Moses takes the People Israel out of Egypt, out of slavery. But the Israelites keep trying to go back. They want to trade in freedom for slavery because they don't know how to be free. They don't know what to do with it.

I probably won't ever win a lottery. I'll probably never be a multimillionaire. But once a week, for one whole day, I pretend I'm one. I spend one day a week doing what I'd do if I won the lottery. I spend one day a week being free. To do this right, I've had to spend some serious time thinking about what to do with my freedom. What's most important to me?

The rules of Judaism teach me, first, what to do with my freedom. And second, they keep me from "going back to Egypt"—from ditching freedom and going back to be a slave.

The rules of Shabbat teach me that family, friends, and community are important. So I spend Shabbat with my family, my friends, and my community. During the work-week, I'm awfully busy. I don't listen to my family and my friends as I should. I don't hear about their lives, their discoveries, their joy. On Shabbat, I take time to listen.

The rules of Shabbat teach me that our ability to enjoy the beauty of nature is one of God's gifts. So I spend part of each Shabbat enjoying nature. I treat nature the way we would treat an artistic masterpiece: I appreciate it, but I don't try to change it. During my workweek, I'm always trying to change things—I'm trying to make things better. On Shabbat, I leave things alone and enjoy them as they are.

The rules of Shabbat teach me to find joy in the moments of my life. On this special day, I don't need possessions to make me happy. Life makes me happy. That's why I stay away from the mall on Shabbat. The mall is all about shopping. The mall says, "The way to be happy is to buy new stuff. You need this new outfit! You need this new makeup! You need this new music!" But Shabbat answers, "Be happy with what you've got! More stuff won't make you happier! Only living better can make you happy!"

All week long, I'm running around getting things done. On Shabbat, I can slow down and really live. On Shabbat, I'm a millionaire, enjoying the freedom I've earned and taking pleasure in the gifts of my life.

Michael isn't convinced. "But Rabbi, what difference does it make if you keep these rules? Is the world going to change if I give up cheeseburgers?"

I know that refusing a cheeseburger is not going to end all the violence in the world. And I know that staying away from the mall on Shabbat is not going to change the belief that stuff makes you happy. My choices may change the world just a little, but they will change *me* a lot. If I'm going to help repair the world, I have to begin by repairing myself. I have to fix the broken parts of me—my violence, my hate, my greed, and my jealousy. I have to live differently, think differently, and look at the world differently. That's the purpose of these rules.

The word for *rule* in Judaism is *mitzvah*. A mitzvah is, literally, God's commandment, God's rule. A mitzvah is God's tool in shaping human beings. A mitzvah teaches me to see the world through God's eyes. A mitzvah teaches me my power to work with God in repairing myself and repairing the world. A mitzvah is a way of teaching me to act Godly.

Keeping kosher is a mitzvah. It teaches me to feel God's love for every living creature.

Observing Shabbat is a mitzvah. It teaches me the preciousness of every moment of time.

Tzedaka, giving charity, is a mitzvah that teaches me the true importance and power of money.

Putting a mezuzah on my door is a mitzvah that teaches me that my home can be a place of holiness.

Judaism has many, many mitzvot, because Judaism's job is ultimately to teach us how to live an important life, how to live with seriousness and with purpose, how to share God's dreams, how to repair ourselves and the world. That's our goal. It's something we work at every day, if we're serious. Just ask Bobby.

9

2 T*Xt Or Not 2 T*Xt?

WHAT'S WRONG WITH TEXTING? WHAT HARM CAN IT DO?

One afternoon, I was a few minutes late for class. To my great relief, everyone was sitting in their seats ready to start. In fact, it was strangely silent in the room. No one talked, there was no conversation.

"Okay, who has a question today?" I asked. But no one answered. In fact, no one even looked up. They were all staring down at their phones, furiously texting, their thumbs flying across the letters.

I waited a moment and then, with more force, I repeated slowly, "I said, does anyone have a question to start our discussion?"

Again, no answer. Just then, Justin looked up. "Oh, hi Rabbi. When did you come in?"

"Everyone look up!" I shouted. "Put the phones away. No texting in class!"

"Come on, Rabbi, what's wrong with texting?" Justin asked. "I've been at school all day, this is my chance to chat with my friends. I'm not bothering anyone, am I? What do you have against texting? Didn't you text your friends when you were a kid?"

When I was your age, texting hadn't been invented. But we had telephones, and my parents allowed me to take my summer earnings and get my own phone installed in my room. Every night, I'd close the door and spend hours talking to friends, near and far. I loved having that connection. But the strange thing was, the more I talked with my friends on the phone, the less I talked with my family. I no longer had time to tell jokes to my brothers, share what happened in school with my parents, or listen to my grandfather's stories, even though we all lived in the same house. As I got closer to my friends using the phone, I got farther from my family.

New technologies have given us remarkable ways to communicate. Telephones, cell phones, e-mail, instant messages, texting, Twitter, and whatever is coming next—they all bring us closer together, but they also push us farther apart. Have you ever been talking to someone when his cell phone rings … and he takes the call, talking on the phone as if you suddenly disappeared? Ever see someone standing in line at the grocery store or waiting at the doctors' office, talking on her phone (often loudly!) as if there was no one else around her?

Texting is a marvelous invention. It connects us instant-ly with friends all over the world. But look at what happened here, just a moment ago. All of you sat in this room together, but you weren't sharing with each other how today went in school, you weren't talking about what happened over the weekend, you weren't listening to each other's thoughts or feelings. You were all focused on your texting, as if each of you were alone in the room. That's my issue with texting—it connects us, but it also pushes us apart because it distracts us from the people who are around us. Texting keeps us from face-to-face conversation with the people who are right here.

In Hebrew, the word for "face" is *panim*. It's related to the Hebrew word *lif'nim*, which means "inside." When I communicate face to face with a person, something special happens—I can perceive their inner life, their thoughts and feelings, what hurts them, what brings them joy. When I look someone in the eye, I come to know that person. I com-municate my care, concern, and respect by looking back at them in a certain way.

When we communicate face to face, we listen in a much deeper way. We listen to what is said, and what isn't said. Try this experiment: Turn on a TV show that's in a lan-guage you don't speak and see how much you can figure out without understanding a word of what is being said. You'll be surprised at how much is communicated by gestures, expressions, tone of voice, or just a look.

From a very early age, we learn to "read" faces. We learn everything about ourselves from watching the faces of those around us. That Hebrew word, *panim,* is a plural noun. It's a strange fact of human existence that not one of us can see his or her own face. The most prominent sign of our identity, and we can't even see it! That means that we need other people to help us know who we are. As young children we learn about ourselves from looking into the faces of those who know us and love us. That's how we learn the most important thing a person can ever learn: That we matter to someone.

In the last century, there lived a great Jewish thinker named Martin Buber who taught that the most important moments in all of life are the moments we meet and communicate deeply with one another. He called these I-Thou moments and taught that everything really good in human life—love, learning, the feeling of being appreciated, knowing that someone really cares for us—comes from these moments of meeting.

Texting is really good for telling your mom you're on your way home for supper, or asking a friend what page the homework is on, or letting your grandmother know you're coming this Sunday. But if you need to say "Thank you" or "I'm sorry" or "I really appreciate you," you need to meet a person face to face. Don't let texting ever get in the way of that kind of sharing.

Jessica raised her hand. "Rabbi, I was listening to you, really! But while you were talking, I got this text from my friend. It's full of really mean things about a girl we know at school. My friend didn't write it, she just forwarded it to me. What should I do?"

"That happens a lot," Jonathan commented. "A kid had to leave my school because someone posted some really terrible stuff about him on Facebook."

Jessica was now paying full attention. "Rabbi, someone could get hurt, just with words! What do we do about that?"

"Sticks and stones can break my bones, but words can never hurt me." When you were young, we taught you to say this little rhyme. As it turns out, it's not true. Words can hurt, sometimes even more than sticks and stones. Rumors, gossip, untruths, half-truths can spread quickly. Everyone wants to know secrets about other people—and everyone just loves to share them! But those words can ruin reputations, push people out of the community, and twist the way people look at and relate to each other. The Talmud teaches that embarrassing another person is a crime worse than murder (Bava Metziah 58b). People can be destroyed by words, and then every time those words are repeated, they are destroyed all over again.

There is a story about a man who went around the community telling lies about the rabbi. When he realized the wrong he had done, he went to the rabbi to apologize and to ask forgiveness. The rabbi told him he would be forgiven, but first he had to do one simple task: Go get a feather pillow, stand in the town square, and cut the pillow open. When he returned to tell the rabbi that he did this, the rabbi asked one more thing: Now, go and gather together all the feathers, and stuff them all back in the pillow. Just like those feathers, you never know how far your destructive words will go. You never know the damage your evil words can cause.

If this is true of spoken words, just imagine how much more true it is with other ways of communicating. An ugly rumor, a vicious story, an embarrassing image can find its way to Facebook, or be forwarded as a text or tweet to many people, without anyone even knowing who it originally came from. Online, people can hide their identity or steal someone's identity, and destroy others by remote control. It's so easy, and so dangerous. Through texts and e-mails, kids are threatened, tormented, and humiliated. And it's serious— kids have lost their lives because of cyber-bullying and Internet cruelty.

If you see this going on, you need to act. First, don't participate. Don't be an accomplice to the destruction of others. Don't forward gossip or cruel messages or images. Tell the sender to stop sending them, then block that sender. Don't visit sites that are aimed at embarrassing, humiliating, or destroying people. Second, get some help. Show these messages to your mom or dad, your teacher, your rabbi. Let them know this is serious and needs to be stopped. (In many places, it's against the law.) If you're the victim of this kind of cruelty, remember there are many people on your side—many people who will protect you. You'll want to respond immediately—to defend yourself—

but don't. Step away from your computer, put down your phone, and get some adult help.

Texting, tweeting, IM'ing, e-mails, websites … these are more than ways of communicating. They have become important elements of our world. Just as we are God's partners in creating the world outside, we are partners in the creation of this new electronic, cyber-space-Internet-iPhone world. It is our responsibility to keep this new world safe for everyone.

10

What Do You See When You Look at Me?

I came into the class one afternoon to find all the boys huddled in the corner around Brian's desk.

"Rabbi, you've got to come see this!" they shouted. I guess it's good to be one of the guys. So I went over to see what was so fascinating.

"Rabbi, can you believe this?!"

It seems that Brian had intercepted a Victoria's Secret catalog from the family mail and brought it to Hebrew School. "Whoa! Is she hot or what?!"

"That is so gross!" moaned the girls from the other side of the room. "How can you let them do that, Rabbi?"

"What's wrong with it?" challenged Josh. "They're just pictures!" Then Josh turned a bit reflective and asked me, "Is there anything wrong with it, Rabbi?"

The question is, what do you see when you look at pictures like that? You're looking at a human being, but you're seeing only their surfaces, their outsides. You don't see a human being; you see a pretty object. Soon enough, these pictures train you to look at real people as objects.

Unfortunately, it's very common for men to look at a woman and notice the shape of her body and the features of her face, and that's all. They forget that there's a person, a self, inside that body and behind that face. They forget that this is a person with her own talents, interests, dreams, and goals—and not just a shapely body and pretty face. And what's even worse is that girls and women begin to look at themselves the same way, evaluating themselves only by their looks. They begin to feel that they're not thin enough, not pretty enough, and therefore not good enough.

The Torah teaches that God created the human being in God's own image, *tzelem eloheem*. This doesn't mean that God looks like us. As we've seen, it means that we carry certain qualities of God—the ability to create, to reason, to care. This is the strongest way the Torah could express the preciousness of each human being and the most powerful way it could demand that we value each person's uniqueness. The second of the Ten Commandments prohibits the making of images of God. So there is only one way to see an image of God in the world: in the character of each human being. When you see a human being, what you're to see is not just a face or a body, and not a pretty object, but a reflection of God.

This includes yourself. Without becoming conceited, it is very important for each of us to recognize how special and important we are. The Rabbis of the Talmud asked: If God wanted to fill the world with people, why in Genesis did God create only one human being? Why not create whole cities and civilizations? They answered: To teach the infinite preciousness and absolute uniqueness of each human being. How precious?

> One who destroys a single life, the Torah considers it as if he destroyed the entire world. And one who saves but a single life, the Torah considers it as if he saved an entire world.... This is an example of the greatness of God. For a human being mints coins with a single stamp, and they all come out looking the same. But God mints all human beings with the stamp of the first man, and yet each is unique. Therefore, every single human being must say, "For my sake, was the whole world created" (*Sanhedrin* 37a).

"Come on, Rabbi, lighten up," Jason complained. "We're just guys having some fun!"

Teenage boys—and even older guys—find pictures like that exciting. It's the way you're wired. But just because you're wired that way doesn't mean you must *behave* that way. You have a higher self—a conscience, the values you've been taught, your internal sense of what's right. And as much as your wiring makes you want to do something, you have the power to choose otherwise.

The Talmud teaches, "Who is strong? One who conquers his impulses" (*Pirke Avot* 4:1). This was written at the time when Roman gladiators fought in arena battles and Roman legions conquered the world. But the Talmud understood that the greatest strength is the strength to control yourself, and the greatest conquest is the conquest of your drives and desires.

Notice, however, that it doesn't say, "One who has no impulses." The Rabbis understood how we're wired. They knew that God created us that way. There are religions that teach that the body and its desires are the source of evil. Not Judaism: In Jewish teaching, the body is a creation of God. The body's impulses and desires aren't evil, but neither are they good. It depends on what you do with them. We have to learn a way not to destroy our impulses but to channel them. We have to learn how to make them expressions of the highest part of ourselves.

Drinking wine can make a person drunk. Or, we can make wine into a symbol of a family gathered to celebrate Shabbat or a holiday, and it becomes kiddush.

Eating just for the sake of survival—like filling a gas tank—is what animals do. Or, we can make a meal a time of sharing and caring and it becomes a holy meal.

Craving money can destroy a person's life and the life of a family. Or, we can use money to repair the world and transform it into *tzedaka*.

Sexual desire, like all the other drives, can poison and destroy a person's life. Or, we can turn it into a symbol of the love, responsibility, and commitment two people share.

It's all a question of how you see yourself. You are a body. But you are not only a body. You carry God's image with you, and you have the power to turn your life into a reflection of God in the world.

CAN I GET A TATTOO OR A PIERCING AND STILL BE JEWISH?

"Boy, did we have a war in my house last night!" Adam announced to the class. "My brother came home from college with a tattoo. My parents freaked out. They said he can't be Jewish anymore! Rabbi, is that true? Can Jews get tattoos?"

"My sister got her nose pierced," Vicki added. "My parents went nuts! Is that also against Judaism?"

Tattoos are not allowed in Judaism, but that doesn't mean your brother isn't Jewish. Your brother is still Jewish. Piercings may not be forbidden, so your sister is also still Jewish. But I can understand why your parents are upset.

Let me ask you a strange question: Who owns your body? Most of us would say that we own our body; after all, who else would own it? But the Jewish tradition teaches a surprising idea—that we don't own our own body. We only borrow it. Our bodies belong to God. When we own something we can take it for granted, and we almost never appreciate how special it is. When we own something, we can abuse it, damage it, or mess it up. But when we borrow something, we take special care. And we try our best to return it in the best condition. In Judaism, we're not permitted to do anything unhealthy or dangerous, anything that might deface or destroy our body, because it's not ours to destroy!

Think about it this way: If you did something destructive to your body, who would suffer? Sure, you would suffer. But how about all the people who love you? They'd suffer too, because you're connected to them. The idea that your body belongs to God means that you are connected to circles of people who love and care for you. Their lives and their happiness depend on you. It's easy to say, "It's my life! It's none of their business!" But the truth is that your decisions affect them, even if you don't see exactly how.

Certainly, getting a tattoo is not the same as taking drugs or smoking or doing something that purposely destroys your body. But if you understand that you don't own your own body, you'll understand why the Torah says no to tattoos. It's like borrowing your friend's car and painting it purple. How would your friend respond when you brought it back? This is what the Torah means when it forbids tattoos: "You shall not make gashes in your flesh for the dead, or make any marks on yourselves: I am the Lord"

(Leviticus 19:28). Why does the rule say, "I am the Lord" at the end? The Rabbis of the Mishna explained that in marking your body, you're messing up what belongs to God (*Mishna Makkot* 3:6).

A tattoo is permanent. (There is a procedure that can remove a tattoo, but it's slow, painful, and doesn't always succeed in putting you back the way you were.) A tattoo is with you forever. It becomes part of you. In most cases, a piercing heals and closes after it's removed. That's why the Torah isn't as opposed to piercings as it is to tattoos. But there is a bigger question to ask about both piercings and tattoos—why get one? Why do you want to do this?

Here's a project: Find a picture of your parents when they were your age. Extra credit if you can find a picture of your grandparents or great-grandparents at your age. Notice anything interesting? Goofy haircuts or strange clothes?

Why did they dress that way? Every generation has its own way of proclaiming, "I'm here and I'm special!" Each generation has its own style: long hair or short hair or weird hair; bell-bottom jeans or skinny jeans or jeans with patches; tiny miniskirts or long, flowing peasant dresses. The difference is that when hairstyles change, you can get a new haircut. When clothing styles change, you can get new clothes. What will people do when tattoos go out of style? And they will, just watch!

Why do people get tattoos and piercings? To say, "I'm here and I'm special!" A piercing or a tattoo is a symbol of individuality. But how special can it be if you're doing just what everyone else is doing? That's what really makes it "cool"—not that it's unique, but it's exactly what everyone else is doing!

If you really want to show that you're an individual, if you really want to say, "I'm here and I'm special," say it through the way you live, through the way you treat people, through the way you think and act. That's original! Make your soul a beautiful symbol of individuality!

11

Why Are There So Many Different Religions? Aren't They All the Same?

"I went to a church last week with my friend from school,"
reported Michelle, a very serious and studious young woman.

"How was it?" I asked her.

"Very, very interesting. Some things were just like our
religion, and some things were very different. Why are there
so many different religions? Aren't all religions the same?"

When I was growing up, I worried that my family wasn't "normal" because we were nothing like the families on TV. Back then, TV families all sat down to eat together in peace, listening to one another in quiet conversation. My family was nothing like that. When we sat down to eat, we were loud: talking, arguing, telling jokes, and sharing stories. Loud! When my Dad asked us what we were learning in school, he really wanted to know. He gave quizzes at the table. You knew your stuff or you didn't get dessert, the best part of the meal.

I used to eat dinner in my friends' homes. I discovered that while no one's family is "normal"—at least not TV normal—each is normal in its own way. Reid's mom was from the South and always cooked up great southern dishes. His family loved sports, so we talked baseball, football, and basketball at the table. At Robert's house, the food was international—spicy and wonderful—and the conversation concentrated on politics and world affairs. Some moms insisted that we sit up straight, keep our elbows off the table, pass our food carefully, and ask permission to leave the table. At my house, the only rule was: Don't stab your brother with your fork.

Every family eats dinner, but each family eats dinner in its own way. Every family has its own "rules of the table," its own stories, its own inside jokes, and its own way of doing things. Similarly, each family has its own way of celebrating birthdays, tucking kids into bed at night, and taking family trips and vacations.

Which way is right? Which is "normal"? Is there one right way to eat dinner? Of course not. It's fascinating to experience all the differences, just as it's great to invite friends to enjoy my family's crazy dinner table, even today.

Religions are like families. Each religion has its own stories, its own ways of celebrating special days, and its own ways of talking to God. Each religion remembers the time when it felt closest to God: Jews remember the Exodus from Egypt, Christians remember the life of Jesus, and

Muslims remember their prophet, Muhammad. By telling our religion's special story, we feel closer to the family of our religion and we feel closer to God. Each religion has its own rituals and symbols for celebrating the special moments of life and the cycle of each year. Each religion has its own ideas about what happens to people after they die, and each has its own ways of responding to the death of a loved one.

Religions also differ in the ideas they teach. Each religion has its own ideas about what makes life worth living, what our job is as human beings, what God is like, and why bad things happen to people. It's worth studying different religions to learn how people across the world and through history have answered these big questions about life. You will discover ideas in other religions that are powerful and interesting. You will discover how your own religion shares some ideas with other religions, and how it offers its own special ways of answering the big questions.

Just as there is not just one right way to "do" dinner, there's no one right way to do religion. But that doesn't make dinner or religion interchangeable any more than our families are interchangeable. I like visiting your home for dinner. Your mom may even be a better cook than mine. But my home is where I belong. In my home, my family shares our special family memories. We tell our family stories and enjoy the things we love to eat. In my religion, we share common memories, stories, and ways of celebrating. I belong to my religion just as I belong to my family.

Some people think the world would be a better place if we did away with all the differences and created one world religion. But that would be like getting rid of all the differences among our families. It would make us all into one big, bland TV family. It's not only impossible to do away with our differences; it would take away an important part of who we are as human beings.

There isn't just one right way to do dinner, and there isn't one right way to do religion. But there are wrong ways. There are families where the table is a battleground—where dinnertime talk is hurtful, abusive, mean, and destructive. There are families where the food isn't shared, so some leave the table full while others leave hungry. There are wrong ways to do dinner, and there are wrong ways to do religion. Using religions to teach hate is wrong. Using religions to destroy human lives and disrespect human rights is wrong. My mom was right. In religion, just as in table manners, there is one basic rule: "Don't stab your brother with a fork."

What Is Christian Religion About? Is It Really That Different from Our Religion?

Michelle told us more about the church service she attended.
"What is Christian religion about, anyway?" asked Josh.
"Is it really that different from our religion?"

Christianity is one of the world's great religions. It has many wise answers for the big questions of life. We live in a country where the vast majority of people are Christian. These are all important reasons why you should take the time to learn about Christianity.

Christianity is a very deep, very old, and very powerful faith. There are many versions of Christian belief and practice. It is very difficult to summarize such a deep tradition in a few moments. But just to get you started, here's a brief description.

Christianity is based on the life and teaching of Jesus, a Jew who lived in Israel during the first century, about two thousand years ago. The story of Jesus is contained in a book Christians call the New Testament, which is part of the Christian Bible. (Our Torah and Prophets are also parts of the Bible Christians use.) Jesus taught a way of coming close to God. He taught this to the Jews of his time. Later, after his death, his followers brought this teaching to those who weren't Jewish. They called it "good news," or "gospel," because it promised that God loves us human beings. Even when we make mistakes, Jesus taught, God still loves us.

After Jesus had become a well-known teacher in the north of Israel, in about the year 30 C.E. (after the year 0) he came to Jerusalem on Passover. In those days, Jews from all over the world made a pilgrimage to celebrate Passover in Jerusalem. This made it the best place to go if you wanted to spread a new religious message. Jerusalem, at that time, was governed by the Romans. The gathering of thousands of Jewish tourists made the Romans, who worried about a possible Jewish revolt, very nervous. As soon as Jesus began preaching his message, he was arrested by the Roman police, tried as a rebel, and executed publicly in a terrifying way—he was hung on a cross until he died. This was the standard way Romans executed criminals, particularly when they wanted to make a public example of someone. Jesus died late on a Friday. Since he couldn't be buried on the Sabbath, his followers placed his body in a tomb. According to the Christian story, when his followers came on Sunday to prepare the body for burial, it was gone. This is viewed as the most important event, known as the resurrection, in the Christian story. According to the story, Jesus later appeared to many of his followers, speaking with them, teaching them, and reassuring them.

Jews can read the stories of Jesus and believe that he was a great teacher. We can appreciate his message and compare it with the message of other Jewish teachers of the time; for example, Hillel. But Christians believe that Jesus was more than a person, more than a great teacher, even more than a prophet. For Christians, this story of returning after death proves that Jesus was much more than human. Christianity teaches that Jesus was a part of God.

The basic Christian idea is that human beings lie, cheat, steal, get angry, hurt one another, and perform endless other evils. That's our human nature. As a result, it is